On top of that, it has safety features to provide you th[e] long unattended hours of dehydration. The COSORI Premium Food Dehydrator has an auto shut-off mechanism that initiates once the timer is up. It also conveniently houses an overheat protection system just in case it detects any overheating during use.

Beginners will love the recipe book that comes with the unit and get them started in no time. Experienced users will appreciate the consistency and reliability of the COSORI dehydrator.

Plus, it comes with a 1-year warranty that can be extended for another year at the buyer's option. One of the best things about getting the COSORI dehydrator is its lifetime assistance and dedication to its patrons.

How Does It Work?

Electric food dehydrators like the COSORI Premium Food Dehydrator are similar to convection ovens since they apply indirect heat to food through hot circulating air.

The main difference is that dehydrators use low heat and requires a longer time to slowly draw out the moisture. Slices of food are placed in trays and stacked vertically to hold more items. The food is laid out individually to make sure that they get even drying.

The heating elements in the dehydrator will heat up the air inside the chamber. Fans will then help the hot air get evenly distributed and slowly dry the food until all moisture is gone. Food items will reduce in size and become crispy as it loses its water content.

Time and temperature are two important factors in dehydration as it requires a slow process to maintain the flavors.

By removing the water content, you are left with flavors that are richer and enhanced. Getting moisture out and exposing food to hot air is also excellent at killing off harmful microorganisms. COSORI also provides a customizable timer and thermostat to let you get the best results each time.

Best Foods to Dehydrate

Fruits

The best fruits to dehydrate are the ones that are in season. You'll be able to get more for a lower price and enjoy them for longer.

It's also a good way to save them from deteriorating. Dehydrate your remaining or overripe stocks to create sweet teas, fruit pies, candy alternatives, healthy chips, and more. Whenever you can, always opt for organic produce to get the maximum health benefits.

Bananas, pineapples, berries, grapes, oranges, peaches, and watermelons are among the best fruits to dehydrate. Just remember to not add any fresh fruit in your current drying batch as it will introduce moisture.

Vegetables

Dried vegetables can be added to your stocks, stews, broths, and soups, especially when they are not available in the market or are expensive. Like fruits, you may also stock up on vegetables that are in season.

Just remember that some vegetables require blanching before dehydrating. Avoid mixing pungent vegetables with those that have milder scents since the circulating air will make these smells stick to the others. You can try carrots, tomatoes, potatoes, celery, mushrooms, corn, chives, cabbage, zucchini, kale, leeks, and more.

Herbs and spices

Store-bought herbs and spices can sometimes be quite expensive. Dehydrate fresh herbs to add to dishes or ground up some seeds to make your own spices. To preserve the natural flavors, oil, and texture, make sure that you don't apply too much heat when dehydrating. 95 degrees F is enough to dehydrate most herbs.

To get the best quality, pick your herbs in the morning just after the dew evaporates. Try drying garlic, onion, basil, mint, chili pepper, oregano, tarragon, cinnamon, and peppercorn.

Meats

Beef jerky from supermarkets is pricey, but if you own a dehydrator, you'll be able to make jerky of any meat you wish. The best meats to dry are those that have little to no fat and are fresh. You may also dehydrate meats that are pre-cooked.

Fish and seafood

Dried fish, shrimp, squid, and shellfish are popular in Asian cuisine. You can stock up on these and add them to soups and dishes to further enhance the taste. Like meats, opt for fish that are low in fat content.

FAQs About Using a Dehydrator

Is it safe to run a dehydrator overnight?

Yes, the COSORI Premium Dehydrator has safety features installed like the automatic shut-off and overheating protection.

What foods cannot be dehydrated?

For safety reasons, never dehydrate meat that has fat in it since it will cause spoilage. Avocados and butter are also not good options for they are mostly fat, and do not sit well when dehydrated. The same is true for nuts and grains that have fat in them.

Is it healthy to eat dehydrated food?

Consuming fresh fruits and vegetables are still your best option if you want to get the maximum amount of nutrient. But since fresh produce has a shorter storage life, it is not always the most practical option for some. Fortunately, their dried counterparts are able to retain most of the vitamins, nutrients, and enzymes, so it surely is a great alternative. Although some nutrients are lost while water is taken out, dehydrated food can still preserve most of the needed vitamins better than any other food preservation methods.

How long will my dehydrated produce last?

If properly dehydrated, dried fruits can last up to 5 years, while vegetables last up to 10. However, it's best practice to use up your dried ingredients between 4 months up to a year.

How do I properly store my dried ingredients?

It is imperative that you store your dehydrated food in airtight containers. Sterilized glass mason jars are a great option, but you may use any container as long as it is properly and tightly sealed.

Vacuum sealing is also excellent at prolonging the shelf-life of your dried food. Freezing them further improves its lifespan. Just make sure that you keep them in a cool and dry place away from direct sunlight, moisture, and air.

Can I use my oven to dehydrate instead of buying a new dehydrator?

Although it is possible to dry food items in an oven, kitchen dehydrators are better at maintaining lower temperatures and circulating the hot air.

These are all essential factors to preserve the natural flavor and nutrient of the food. Dehydrators are much more efficient and provide reliable and consistent results than using a traditional oven.

Are dehydrators noisy when operated?

The COSORI Premium Food Dehydrator is a surprisingly quiet appliance and does not have any annoying sounds when it is running a cycle.

Do dehydrators really remove any bacteria in the food?

By removing the water content in the food, microorganisms like bacteria can no longer multiply or survive. For raw meats that you are planning to dehydrate, make sure that you apply high heat or about 160 degrees Fin the beginning before bringing it down to 145 degrees F.

Can I only dry food in the dehydrator?

Dehydrators are versatile appliances. You don't have to limit your use to edibles alone. Fruits peels and fragrant flowers can be dried up to make potpourri too. Basically, you can safely use items that you would normally sun dry. Some people have used their dehydrators to dry seeds, jewelry, clay, crafts, cake decorations, paper mache, fire starters, and even dog treats.

Does the process of dehydration also increase the sugars in food?

The sugar content remains the same as the fresh fruit, and dehydration does not augment it. Dried ripe fruits will become much sweeter since the water content was eliminated, leaving you with a more concentrated flavor within a smaller mass.

Is there a way to prevent dried food from browning?

Yes. Browning is the natural reaction of some produce to oxidation. Soaking or spraying your cut fruits with a solution of water and either citric acid, ascorbic acid, or sulfites will prevent it from browning during the process. If you don't have access to any of these, try using a solution of 2 quarts of water and ½ cup of lemon juice. Do not use this solution to fragile leafy greens as it will burn its leaves.

Chapter 2: Meat

Beef Jerky

Preparation Time: 12 hours and 10 minutes
Dehydration Time: 6 hours
Servings: 4

Ingredients:

- 2 lb. beef eye of round
- ½ cup soy sauce
- ½ cup Worcestershire sauce
- 1 teaspoon salt
- 1 tablespoon honey

Method:

1. Slice the beef eye of round across the grain.
2. Add the soy sauce, Worcestershire sauce, salt and honey in a sealable plastic bag.
3. Add the beef to the plastic bag.
4. Turn to coat.
5. Place inside the refrigerator for 12 hours.
6. Drain the marinade.
7. Add the beef to the Cosori Premium Food Dehydrator.
8. Process at 165 degrees F for 6 hours.

Storage Tips: Store in a cool dry place. Store in a glass jar with lid for up to 2 weeks.

Preparation & Dehydration Tips: Slices should be about 5 mm thick.

Candied Bacon

Preparation Time: 12 hours and 10 minutes
Dehydration Time: 6 hours
Servings: 4

Ingredients:

- 10 slices bacon
- 3 tablespoons brown sugar
- 3 tablespoons soy sauce
- 2 teaspoons mirin
- 2 teaspoons sesame oil
- 2 tablespoons chili garlic sauce

Method:

1. Slice each bacon strip into 3 portions.
2. Add the rest of the ingredients in a bowl.
3. Mix well.
4. Add the bacon slices in the mixture.
5. Cover and refrigerate for 12 hours.
6. Add the bacon to the Cosori Premium Food Dehydrator.
7. Dehydrate at 165 degrees F for 6 hours.

Storage Tips: Store candied bacon in a glass jar with lid for up to 2 weeks.

Preparation & Dehydration Tips: Add chili powder to the marinade if you want your candied bacon extra spicy.

Beef Teriyaki Jerky

Preparation Time: 12 hours and 10 minutes
Dehydration Time: 6 hours
Servings: 4

Ingredients:

- 2 lb. beef round, sliced
- ¼ cup brown sugar
- ½ cup soy sauce
- ¼ cup pineapple juice
- 1 clove garlic, crushed
- ¼ teaspoon ginger, grated

Method:

1. Add all the ingredients in a bowl.
2. Mix well.
3. Transfer to a sealable plastic bag.
4. Add the beef to the plastic bag.
5. Marinate in the refrigerator for 12 hours.
6. Discard the marinade before dehydrating.
7. Add to the Cosori Premium Food Dehydrator.
8. Process at 165 degrees F for 6 hours.

Storage Suggestions: Keep in a glass jar with lid or vacuum sealed bag.

Preparation & Dehydration Tips: Beef should be sliced at least 5 mm thick.

Vietnamese Beef Jerky

Preparation Time: 12 hours and 10 minutes
Dehydration Time: 6 hours
Servings: 4

Ingredients:

- 2 lb. beef round
- 3 tablespoons fish sauce
- 1 tablespoon soy sauce
- 2 tablespoons lime juice
- ¼ cup brown sugar

Method:

1. Combine all the ingredients in a bowl.
2. Transfer to a sealable plastic bag.
3. Turn to coat the beef strips evenly with the marinade.
4. Place in the refrigerator for 12 hours.
5. Drain the marinade.
6. Add the beef to the Cosori Premium Food Dehydrator.
7. Process at 165 degrees F for 6 hours.

Storage Suggestions: Store the jerky in a glass jar with lid for up to 1 week.

Preparation & Dehydration Tips: Slice the beef across the grain. Make sure beef is at least 5 mm thick.

Smoked Herbed Bacon Jerky

Preparation Time: 10 minutes
Dehydration Time: 6 hours
Servings: 4

Ingredients:

- 10 slices smoked bacon
- 1 teaspoon ground fennel seeds
- 1/8 teaspoon onion powder
- 1/8 teaspoon garlic powder
- ¼ teaspoon dried sage
- ¼ teaspoon dried thyme
- 1 teaspoon brown sugar
- ¼ teaspoon red pepper flakes
- 1/8 teaspoon black pepper

Method:

1. Slice the bacon into 3 portions.
2. In a bowl, mix the rest of the ingredients.
3. Sprinkle both sides of the bacon with the seasoning mixture.
4. Add the bacon slices to the Cosori Premium Food Dehydrator.
5. Dehydrate at 165 degrees F for 6 hours.

Storage Suggestions: Store the bacon jerky in a glass jar with lid for up to 1 week.

Preparation & Dehydration Tips: You can add more red pepper flakes if you want the jerky to be spicier.

Pork Jerky in Chipotle Sauce

Preparation Time: 12 hours and 10 minutes
Dehydration Time: 6 hours
Servings: 2

Ingredients:

- 1 tablespoon tomato paste
- 7 oz. chipotle adobo sauce
- 1 teaspoon salt
- 1 teaspoon sugar
- 1 teaspoon garlic powder
- 1 lb. pork tenderloin, sliced

Method:

1. Mix the tomato paste, chipotle adobo sauce, salt, sugar and garlic powder in a bowl.
2. Transfer to a sealable plastic bag along with the pork tenderloin slices.
3. Seal and refrigerate for 12 hours.
4. Drain the marinade.
5. Add the pork slices to the Cosori Premium Food Dehydrator.
6. Process at 158 degrees F for 6 hours.

Storage Suggestions: Place in a glass jar with lid. Store in a cool dry place, away from sunlight.

Preparation & Dehydration Tips: Pork tenderloin should be sliced at least 5 mm thick.

Paprika Pork Jerky

Preparation Time: 12 hours and 10 minutes
Dehydration Time: 6 hours
Servings: 2

Ingredients:

- 1 lb. pork tenderloin, sliced
- ½ cup ketchup
- 1 teaspoon onion powder
- 1 teaspoon garlic powder
- 1 teaspoon smoked paprika
- 1 teaspoon ground mustard
- 1 teaspoon chili powder
- Salt and pepper to taste

Method:

1. Add the ketchup to a bowl.
2. Stir in the onion powder, garlic powder, paprika, mustard, chili powder, salt and pepper.
3. Mix well.
4. Transfer the mixture to a sealable plastic bag.
5. Add the pork to the plastic bag.
6. Seal and refrigerate for 12 hours.
7. Remove the pork from the marinade.
8. Add to the Cosori Premium Food Dehydrator.
9. Dry at 158 degrees F for 6 hours.

Storage Suggestions: Store the pork jerky in a glass jar with lid. Store in a cool dry place for up to 2 weeks.

Preparation & Dehydration Tips: You can also use garlic salt in place of garlic powder and salt.

Beef Bulgogi Jerky

Preparation Time: 12 hours and 10 minutes
Dehydration Time: 6 hours
Servings: 4

Ingredients:

- 2 lb. beef round, sliced
- 4 tablespoons brown sugar
- 4 tablespoons soy sauce
- 1 tablespoon garlic powder
- 1 tablespoon sesame oil
- Sal to taste

Method:

1. Place the beef inside a sealable plastic bag.
2. In a bowl, mix the remaining ingredients.
3. Add the mixture to the plastic bag.
4. Place the beef in the refrigerator for 12 hours.
5. Drain the marinade.
6. Add the beef to the Cosori Premium Food Dehydrator.
7. Set at 165 degrees F.
8. Process for 6 hours.

Storage Suggestions: Place in a glass jar with lid and store in a cool, dry place.

Preparation & Dehydration Tips: Slice the beef across the grain. Each slice should be at least 5 mm thick.

Mustard Beef Jerky with Balsamic Vinegar

Preparation Time: 12 hours and 10 minutes
Dehydration Time: 6 hours
Servings: 4

Ingredients:

- 2 lb. beef round, sliced
- 2 tablespoons olive oil
- 1 tablespoon Dijon mustard
- 1 cup balsamic vinegar
- 2 garlic cloves, crushed
- 1 teaspoon salt

Method:

1. Add the beef to a sealable plastic bag.
2. Combine the rest of the ingredients in a bowl.
3. Mix well.
4. Pour the mixture into the plastic bag.
5. Place in the refrigerator for 12 hours.
6. Drain the marinade.
7. Add the beef slices to the Cosori Premium Food Dehydrator.
8. Set the dehydrator to 165 degrees F.
9. Dry for 6 hours.

Storage Suggestions: Keep the beef jerky slices in a glass container with lid. Store in an area away from sunlight.

Preparation & Dehydration Tips: You can dehydrate longer for up to 8 hours.

Buffalo Jerky

Preparation Time: 15 hours and 10 minutes
Dehydration Time: 6 hours
Servings: 4

Ingredients:

- 2 lb. beef round, sliced
- 1 teaspoon salt
- 1 cup buffalo sauce

Method:

1. Season the beef slices with the salt.
2. Add the buffalo sauce to a bowl.
3. Stir in the seasoned beef.
4. Cover the bowl.
5. Refrigerate for 15 hours.
6. Drain the marinade.
7. Add the beef slices to the Cosori Premium Food Dehydrator.
8. Process at 165 degrees F for 6 hours.

Storage Suggestions: Place the beef jerky in a sealable glass container. Store for up to 2 weeks.

Preparation & Dehydration Tips: You can also add hot sauce to the marinade for extra zing.

Barbecue Beef Jerky

Preparation Time: 12 hours and 10 minutes
Dehydration Time: 6 hours
Servings: 4

Ingredients:

- 2 lb. beef round, sliced
- Salt and pepper to taste
- 2 teaspoons dried oregano
- 2 teaspoons ground cumin
- 1 teaspoon onion powder
- 1 teaspoon ground coriander
- 4 cloves garlic, grated
- ½ cup olive oil
- ½ cup lime juice
- 1 teaspoon red pepper flakes

Method:

1. Add the beef slices to a sealable plastic bag.
2. In a bowl, mix the salt, pepper, herbs, spices, garlic, olive oil, lime juice and red pepper flakes.
3. Pour mixture into the plastic bag.
4. Turn to coat beef slices evenly with the mixture.
5. Seal and marinate for 12 hours.
6. Drain the marinade.
7. Place the beef slices to the Cosori Food Dehydrator Dehydrator.
8. Set it to 165 degrees F and process for 6 hours.

Storage Suggestions: Keep the beef jerky in a vacuum sealed plastic bag.

Preparation & Dehydration Tip: You can also use lemon juice instead of lime juice.

Sweet & Sour Pork

Preparation Time: 12 hours and 10 minutes
Dehydration Time: 6 hours
Servings: 4

Ingredients:

- 1 lb. pork tenderloin, sliced
- 2 tablespoons fish sauce
- ¼ cup lime juice
- ¼ cup brown sugar
- 1 shallot, grated
- 2 garlic cloves, grated
- Salt and pepper to taste

Method:

1. Combine all the ingredients in a bowl.
2. Mix well.
3. Transfer to a sealable plastic bag.
4. Chill in the refrigerator for 12 hours.
5. Remove from the marinade.
6. Transfer the pork slices to the Cosori Premium Food Dehydrator.
7. Process at 158 degrees F for 6 hours.

Storage Suggestions: Store in a glass jar with lid, away from direct sunlight.

Preparation & Dehydration Tips: See to it that the slices are at least 5 mm thick.

Lamb Jerky

Preparation Time: 13 hours
Dehydration Time: 6 hours
Servings: 4

Ingredients:

- 3 lb. leg of lamb, sliced
- ¼ cup soy sauce
- 3 tablespoons Worcestershire sauce
- 1 tablespoon oregano
- 1 teaspoon garlic powder
- 1 1/2 teaspoons onion powder
- Pepper to taste

Method:

1. Add the lamb slices to a sealable plastic bag.
2. Combine the remaining ingredients in a bowl.
3. Mix well.
4. Pour the mixture into a sealable plastic bag.
5. Marinate in the refrigerator for 13 hours.
6. Place the lamb slices to the Cosori Premium Food Dehydrator.
7. Process at 145 degrees F for 6 hours.

Storage Suggestions: Store the lamb jerky in a glass jar with lid for up to 2 weeks.

Preparation & Dehydration Tips: Freeze the lamb for 1 hour first so it will be easier to slice into strips.

Lemon Fish Jerky

Preparation Time: 4 hours and 10 minutes
Dehydration Time: 8 hours
Servings: 2

Ingredients:

- 1 lb. cod fillet, sliced
- 1 tablespoon lemon juice
- 1 teaspoon lemon zest
- 2 tablespoons olive oil
- 1 teaspoon dill
- 1 clove garlic, grated
- Salt to taste

Method:

1. Combine the fish slices and the rest of the ingredients in a sealable plastic bag.
2. Turn to coat the fish evenly with the marinade.
3. Place the plastic bag inside the refrigerator for 4 hours.
4. Drain the marinade.
5. Add the fish slices to the Cosori Premium Food Dehydrator.
6. Process at 145 degrees F for 8 hours.

Storage Suggestions: Store the fish jerky in a glass jar with lid or vacuum sealed bag for up to 2 weeks.

Preparation & Dehydration Tips: You can also use salmon for this recipe.

Salmon Jerky

Preparation Time: 4 hours and 10 minutes
Dehydration Time: 8 hours
Servings: 2

Ingredients:

- 1 ¼ lb. salmon, sliced
- ½ cup soy sauce
- 1 tablespoon molasses
- 1 tablespoon lemon juice
- Pepper to taste

Method:

1. Place the salmon slices in a sealable plastic bag.
2. Combine the rest of the ingredients in a bowl.
3. Add the mixture to the plastic bag.
4. Marinate inside the refrigerator for 4 hours.
5. Drain the marinade.
6. Add the salmon slices to the Cosori Premium Food Dehydrator
7. Process at 145 degrees F for 8 hours.

Storage Suggestions: Place the fish jerky in a food container with lid. Store for up to 2 weeks.

Preparation & Dehydration Tips: Use freshly squeezed lemon juice. Salmon slices should be ¼ inch thick.

Fish Teriyaki Jerky

Preparation Time: 4 hours and 10 minutes
Dehydration Time: 8 hours
Servings: 2

Ingredients:

- 1 lb. salmon, sliced
- ¼ teaspoon ginger, grated
- ¼ cup sugar
- ½ cup soy sauce
- ¼ cup orange juice
- 1 clove garlic, minced

Method:

1. Combine all the ingredients in a bowl.
2. Mix well.
3. Transfer to a sealable plastic bag.
4. Seal and refrigerate for 4 hours.
5. Drain the marinade.
6. Add the salmon to the Cosori Premium Food Dehydrator.
7. Process at 145 degrees F for 8 hours.

Storage Suggestions: Store the salmon jerky in a glass jar with lid.

Preparation & Dehydration Tips: You can process longer in the dehydrator if you want the fish slices crispier and dryer.

Cajun Fish Jerky

Preparation Time: 4 hours and 10 minutes
Dehydration Time: 8 hours
Servings: 2

Ingredients:

- 1 teaspoon garlic powder
- 1 teaspoon paprika
- 1 teaspoon onion powder
- ¼ teaspoon cayenne pepper
- 1 tablespoon lemon juice
- Salt and pepper to taste
- 1 lb. cod fillet, sliced

Method:

1. Mix the spices, lemon juice, salt and pepper in a bowl.
2. Season the fish with this mixture.
3. Transfer the seasoned fish and marinade in a sealable plastic bag.
4. Marinate in the refrigerator for 4 hours.
5. Drain the marinade.
6. Arrange the salmon slices on the Cosori Premium Food Dehydrator.
7. Process at 145 degrees F for 8 hours.

Storage Suggestions: Store in a vacuum sealed plastic bag or glass jar with lid.

Preparation & Dehydration Tips: You can use other white fish fillet for this recipe.

Venison Jerky

Preparation Time: 1 day and 30 minutes
Dehydration Time: 4 hours
Servings: 2

Ingredients:

- 1 lb. venison roast, silver skin trimmed and sliced thinly
- 4 tablespoons coconut amino
- ¼ teaspoon onion powder
- ¼ teaspoon garlic powder
- ¼ teaspoon red pepper flakes
- 1 tablespoon honey
- 4 tablespoons Worcestershire sauce
- Salt and pepper to taste

Method:

1. Place the venison roast slices in a bowl.
2. In another bowl, combine the rest of the ingredients.
3. Pour this mixture into the first bowl.
4. Stir to coat meat evenly with the mixture.
5. Cover the bowl.
6. Chill in the refrigerator for 1 day, stirring every 3 or 4 hours.
7. Drain the marinade.
8. Place the venison slices in the Cosori Premium Food Dehydrator.
9. Process at 160 degrees F for 4 hours.

Storage Suggestions: Store in vacuum sealed bags for up to 3 months or in ziplock bags for up to 2 weeks.

Preparation & Dehydration Tips: Freeze the venison meat for 1 hour before slicing.

Hickory Smoked Jerky

Preparation Time: 12 hours and 10 minutes
Dehydration Time: 4 hours
Servings: 4

Ingredients:

- 1 lb. beef round, sliced
- ½ cup hickory smoked marinade
- ¼ cup barbecue sauce
- 2 tablespoons brown sugar
- 1 teaspoon onion powder
- Pinch cayenne pepper
- Salt and pepper to taste

Method:

1. Place the beef slices in a sealable plastic bag.
2. In a bowl, combine the marinade, barbecue sauce, sugar, onion powder, cayenne, salt and pepper.
3. Pour the mixture into the bag.
4. Seal and marinate in the refrigerator for 12 hours.
5. Discard the marinade and add the beef to the Cosori Premium Food Dehydrator.
6. Process at 180 degrees F for 4 hours, flipping halfway through.

Storage Suggestions: Store in a glass jar with lid for up to 2 weeks.

Preparation & Dehydration Tips: Arrange the meat in a single layer without overlapping.

Beer Beef Jerky

Preparation Time: 6 hours and 10 minutes
Dehydration Time: 5 hours
Servings: 2

Ingredients:

- 1 lb. beef round, sliced
- ½ cup soy sauce
- 2 cloves garlic, minced
- 2 cups beer
- 1 tablespoon liquid smoke
- 1 tablespoon honey
- Pepper to taste

Method:

1. Add the beef to a sealable plastic bag.
2. Combine the rest of the ingredients in a bowl.
3. Pour the mixture into the bag.
4. Seal and refrigerate for 6 hours.
5. Drain the marinade.
6. Place the beef in the Cosori Premium Food Dehydrator.
7. Dehydrate at 160 degrees F for 1 hour.
8. Reduce temperature to 150 degrees F and process for additional 4 hours.

Storage Suggestions: Store in a food container with lid for up to 2 weeks.

Preparation & Dehydration Tips: Make sure beef is trimmed of fat before dehydrating.

Chapter 3: Fruits

Honey Peaches with Bourbon

Preparation Time: 4 hours and 10 minutes
Dehydration Time: 16 hours
Servings: 1

Ingredients:

- 1 peach, cored and sliced
- ¼ cup honey
- ¼ cup hot water
- 3 tablespoons bourbon

Method:

1. Add the slices to a sealable plastic bag.
2. In a glass bowl, mix the honey and hot water.
3. Mix until the honey has been dissolved.
4. Pour in the bourbon.
5. Let cool.
6. Once cool, add this to the plastic bag.
7. Marinate for 4 hours.
8. Drain the marinade.
9. Add these to the Cosori Premium Food Dehydrator.
10. Dehydrate at 145 degrees F for 16 hours.

Storage Suggestions: Pack in a sealable plastic bag for up to 10 days.

Preparation & Dehydration Tips: You can also skip the bourbon and marinate in honey only.

Raspberry Rolls

Preparation Time: 10 minutes
Dehydration Time: 5 hours
Servings: 4

Ingredients:

- 1 ½ lb. raspberries
- 2 tablespoons sugar

Method:

1. Add the raspberries and sugars to a blender.
2. Blend until smooth.
3. Strain to remove the seeds.
4. Add the pureed raspberry back to the blender.
5. Blend until the mixture has turned into liquid.
6. Add the liquid to a fruit roll sheet.
7. Place these in the Cosori Premium Food Dehydrator.
8. Dehydrate at 165 degrees F for 5 hours.

Storage Suggestions: Store in a glass jar with lid in a cool dry place.

Preparation & Dehydration Tips: You can also use strawberries or blueberries to make this recipe.

Blackberry Tuile

Preparation Time: 10 minutes
Dehydration Time: 3 hours
Servings: 4

Ingredients:

- 1 ½ lb. blackberries
- 2 tablespoons white sugar

Method:

1. Process the blackberries and sugar in a blender.
2. Strain the mixture to remove the seeds.
3. Add the mixture to the blender.
4. Process on high speed.
5. Pour the fruit liquid into a fruit roll sheet.
6. Place these in the Cosori Premium Food Dehydrator.
7. Dehydrate at 165 degrees F for 3 hours.

Storage Suggestions: Store in a food container with lid, away from direct sunlight.

Preparation & Dehydration Tips: You can also slice the blackberries first and remove the seeds so you only have to blend it once.

Fruit Leather

Preparation Time: 30 minutes
Dehydration Time: 8 hours
Servings: 4

Ingredients:

- 3 peaches, sliced
- 3 apricots, sliced
- 1 tablespoon sugar

Method:

1. Put the peaches and apricots in a pot over medium low heat.
2. Sprinkle with sugar.
3. Mix well.
4. Cook for 10 minutes.
5. Let cool.
6. Transfer to a blender.
7. Blend on low speed until pureed.
8. Pour the mixture into a fruit roll sheet.
9. Place the roll sheet in the Cosori Premium Food Dehydrator.
10. Dehydrate at 165 degrees F or 8 hours.

Storage Suggestions: Arrange the solidified fruits on a baking tray and let it sit for a few minutes before storing in a food container.

Preparation & Dehydration Tips: You can also dehydrate for up to 12 hours to obtain drier results.

Cinnamon Apple Chips

Preparation Time: 10 minutes
Dehydration Time: 12 hours
Servings: 4

Ingredients:

- 2 apples, sliced thinly
- 1 tablespoon white sugar
- 1 tablespoon lemon juice
- ¼ teaspoon nutmeg
- ½ teaspoon vanilla extract
- 1 teaspoon ground cinnamon

Method:

1. Combine all the ingredients in a bowl.
2. Coat the apples slices evenly with the mixture.
3. Arrange the apple slices in the Cosori Premium Food Dehydrator.
4. Dehydrate at 145 degrees F for 6 hours.

Storage Suggestions: Store in a glass jar with lid.

Preparation & Dehydration Tips: Apple slices should be at least ¼ inch thick.

Plum & Grape Fruit Leather

Preparation Time: 20 minutes
Dehydration Time: 12 hours
Servings: 4

Ingredients:

- 2 cups red grapes (seedless)
- 5 plums, sliced
- 2 tablespoons sugar

Method:

1. Put all the ingredients in a pot over medium low heat.
2. Cook for 15 minutes.
3. Transfer the mixture to a blender.
4. Blend until smooth.
5. Pour the mixture into a fruit roll sheet.
6. Place in the Cosori Premium Food Dehydrator.
7. Process at 165 degrees F for 12 hours.

Storage Suggestions: Dry the fruit leather on a tray after dehydrating and before storing.

Preparation & Dehydration Tips: You can also process for 8 hours only.

Berry Fruit Leather

Preparation Time: 10 minutes
Dehydration Time: 10 hours
Servings: 4

Ingredients:

- 1 lb. strawberries
- ½ cup raspberries
- 1 teaspoon vanilla extract

Method:

1. Process all the ingredients in a blender.
2. Pulse until smooth.
3. Strain to remove seeds.
4. Put the mixture back to the blender.
5. Pulse until liquified.
6. Pour the fruit puree into a fruit roll sheet and place in the Cosori Premium Food Dehydrator.
7. Dehydrate at 165 degrees F for 10 hours.

Storage Suggestions: Sprinkle with white sugar before storing in a glass jar.

Preparation & Dehydration Tips: You can also use other berries for this recipe.

Dried Mangoes

Preparation Time: 15 minutes
Dehydration Time: 12 hours
Servings: 2

Ingredients:

- 2 mangoes, sliced thinly
- 2 tablespoons honey
- 3 teaspoons lemon juice

Method:

1. Marinate the mangoes in honey and lemon juice for 15 minutes.
2. Transfer mango slices in the Cosori Premium Food Dehydrator.
3. Dry at 165 degrees F for 12 hours.

Storage Suggestions: Store in a glass jar with lid away from direct sunlight.

Preparation & Dehydration Tips: You can add more honey if you want your dried mangoes sweeter.

Blackberry & Blueberry Fruit Rolls

Preparation Time: 10 minutes
Dehydration Time: 9 hours
Servings: 4

Ingredients:

- 1 lb. blueberries
- 1 cup blackberries

Method:

1. Add the berries to a blender.
2. Blend on low speed until fully combined.
3. Strain the mixture and remove the seeds.
4. Put the mixture back to the blender.
5. Pulse until the mixture has turned into liquid.
6. Pour the mixture into a fruit roll sheet and place in the Cosori Premium Food Dehydrator.
7. Process at 165 degrees F for 9 hours.

Storage Suggestions: Keep the fruit leather in a sealed plastic bag or in a glass jar with lid.

Preparation & Dehydration Tips: You can also add a teaspoon sugar to the mixture if you want your fruit rolls sweeter.

Choco Bananas

Preparation Time: 15 minutes
Dehydration Time: 16 hours
Servings: 2

Ingredients:

- 1 banana, sliced thinly
- 4 oz. chocolate chips
- Sea salt

Method:

1. Arrange the banana slices in the Cosori Premium Food Dehydrator.
2. Process at 145 degrees F for 16 hours.
3. In a pan over medium low heat, melt the chocolate for 5 to 10 minutes.
4. Dip the dried bananas in the chocolate.
5. Sprinkle with the sea salt.

Storage Suggestions: Wait for the chocolate to harden before storing the treats in a glass jar with lid.

Preparation & Dehydration Tips: Make sure that the banana slices do not overlap in the food dehydrator.

Dried Strawberries

Preparation Time: 10 minutes
Dehydration Time: 8 hours
Servings: 4

Ingredients:

- 1 lb. strawberries, sliced

Method:

1. Place the strawberry slices in the Cosori Premium Food Dehydrator.
2. Process at 135 degrees F for 8 hours.

Storage Suggestions: Keep in a glass jar with lid.

Preparation & Dehydration Tips: Hull and slice the strawberries before dehydrating them. Slices should be 1/8 inch thick.

Hazelnut Banana Leather

Preparation Time: 5 minutes
Dehydration Time: 3 hours
Servings: 2

Ingredients:

- 2 bananas, sliced
- Chocolate hazelnut spread

Method:

1. Combine the bananas and chocolate hazelnut spread in your food processor.
2. Pulse until smooth.
3. Form round shapes of about ¼ inch thick on parchment paper.
4. Transfer to the Cosori Premium Food Dehydrator.
5. Process at 125 degrees F for 4 hours.

Storage Suggestions: Store in a glass jar with lid. Place jar in a cool dry place.

Preparation & Dehydration Tips: The treats should no longer be sticky when touched.

Apple Fruit Leather

Preparation Time: 10 minutes
Dehydration Time: 6 hours
Servings: 2

Ingredients:

- 2 cups applesauce
- 2 cups sweet potatoes, cooked and mashed
- ¼ cup honey
- 1 teaspoon cinnamon
- Salt to taste

Method:

1. Add all the ingredients to a blender.
2. Pulse until smooth.
3. Add the mixture to fruit roll sheets and place in the Cosori Premium Food Dehydrator.
4. Dry at 100 degrees F for 6 hours.

Storage Suggestions: Store apple leather in a sealable plastic bag.

Preparation & Dehydration Tips: You can also add a little lemon juice to the mixture to balance the flavor.

Peanut Butter & Banana Leather

Preparation Time: 5 minutes
Dehydration Time: 4 hours
Servings: 2

Ingredients:

- 2 bananas, sliced
- 2 tablespoons peanut butter

Method:

1. Process bananas and peanut butter in a food processor for 1 minute.
2. Spread a layer of the mixture onto the dehydrator sheet.
3. Dry at 135 degrees F for 4 hours.

Storage Suggestions: Slice the leather before storing.

Preparation & Dehydration Tips: You can also add melted chocolate into the mixture if you like.

Dried Apple Chips with Cinnamon

Preparation Time: 15 hours
Dehydration Time: 10 hours
Servings: 2

Ingredients:

- 2 apples, sliced
- 1 tablespoon lemon juice
- 2 teaspoons cinnamon powder

Method:

1. Drizzle the apple slices with lemon juice.
2. Arrange the apple slices in the Cosori Premium Food Dehydrator.
3. Process at 135 degrees F for 10 hours.
4. Sprinkle with the cinnamon before serving.

Storage Suggestions: Store in a glass jar with lid.

Preparation & Dehydration Tips: You can also keep the apple peel if you like but scrub the peel first with apple cider vinegar before processing.

Candied Pumpkin

Preparation Time: 15 minutes
Dehydration Time: 8 hours
Servings: 2

Ingredients:

- 1 cup coconut milk
- 2 cups applesauce
- 2 cups pumpkin puree
- ¼ cup honey
- ½ teaspoon ground allspice
- ½ teaspoon ground nutmeg
- 1 teaspoon ground cinnamon
- ¼ cup coconut flakes
- 2 tablespoons dried cranberries, chopped

Method:

1. Combine all the ingredients in a bowl.
2. Spread the mixture in the fruit leather sheet of your Cosori Premium Food Dehydrator.
3. Dehydrate at 135 degrees F for 8 hours.

Storage Suggestions: Slice the fruit leather before storing in a food container with lid.

Preparation & Dehydration Tips: Grease the fruit leather sheet with a little bit of oil before processing.

Orange Fruit Leather

Preparation Time: 10 minutes
Dehydration Time: 6 hours
Servings: 4

Ingredients:

- 1 cup applesauce
- 1 cup orange juice concentrate
- 32 oz. vanilla yogurt

Method:

1. Add all the ingredients in your blender.
2. Pulse until smooth.
3. Spread the mixture onto the roll sheet.
4. Dry at 135 degrees F for 6 hours.

Storage Suggestions: Store in an airtight food container for up to 2 weeks.

Preparation & Dehydration Tips: Grease the roll sheet with a little olive oil before processing.

Dried Lemon

Preparation Time: 5 minutes
Dehydration Time: 10 hours
Servings: 2

Ingredients:

- 2 lemons, sliced

Method:

1. Arrange the lemon slices in the Cosori Premium Food Dehydrator.
2. Dry the lemon at 125 degrees F for 10 hours.

Storage Suggestions: Store in an airtight container.

Preparation & Dehydration Tips: Drizzle with honey before drying if you like them a little sweeter.

Dried Papaya Cubes

Preparation Time: 10 minutes
Dehydration Time: 12 hours
Servings: 4

Ingredients:

- 2 papaya, diced

Method:

1. Add the diced papaya to the Cosori Premium Food Dehydrator.
2. Process at 135 degrees F for 12 hours.

Storage Suggestions: Store in an airtight jar.

Preparation & Dehydration Tips: You can also sprinkle with sugar before dehydrating.

Dried Kiwi

Preparation Time: 15 minutes
Dehydration Time: 12 hours
Servings: 2

Ingredients:

- 2 kiwis, peeled and sliced thinly

Method:

1. Place the kiwi slices in the Cosori Premium Food Dehydrator.
2. Dry at 135 degrees F for 12 hours.

Storage Suggestions: Store in a glass jar with lid. Place the jar in a cool dry place.

Preparation & Dehydration Tips: Kiwi slices should be at least 6mm thick.

Chapter 4: Vegetables

Dried Cauliflower Popcorn

Preparation Time: 15 minutes
Dehydration Time: 8 hours
Serving: 1

Ingredients:

- 2 cups cauliflower florets
- 4 tablespoons hot sauce
- 3 tablespoons coconut oil
- 1 teaspoon smoked cayenne
- ½ teaspoon ground cumin
- 1 tablespoons paprika

Method:

1. Toss the cauliflower florets in hot sauce and coconut oil.
2. Sprinkle with the smoked cayenne, cumin and paprika.
3. Add the seasoned cauliflower to the Cosori Premium Food Dehydrator.
4. Dry at 130 degrees F for 8 hours.

Storage Suggestions: Store in an airtight plastic bag.

Preparation & Dehydration Tips: Add more cayenne pepper for spicier cauliflower popcorn.

Zucchini Snacks

Preparation Time: 45 minutes
Dehydration Time: 12 hours
Servings: 4

Ingredients:

- 8 zucchinis, sliced into rounds and seeds removed
- 1 cup grape juice concentrate
- 1 cup water

Method:

1. Add all the ingredients to a pot over medium heat.
2. Bring to a boil.
3. Reduce heat and simmer for 30 minutes.
4. Drain the zucchini and let cool.
5. Add the zucchinis to the Cosori Premium Food Dehydrator.
6. Process at 135 degrees F for 12 hours.

Storage Suggestions: Store in the refrigerator for up to 1 week.

Preparation & Dehydration Tips: Do not overcook the zucchinis.

Cucumber Chips

Preparation Time: 15 minutes
Dehydration Time: 10 hours
Servings: 6

Ingredients:

- 3 cucumber, sliced into rounds
- 1 tablespoon avocado oil
- 2 teaspoons apple cider vinegar
- Salt to taste

Method:

1. Toss the cucumber slices in avocado oil and vinegar.
2. Season with the salt.
3. Add the cucumber slices to the Cosori Premium Food Dehydrator.
4. Dehydrate at 135 degrees F for 10 hours.

Storage Suggestions: Store in an airtight container.

Preparation & Dehydration Tips: You can use a mandoline slicer to slice the cucumbers thinly. Dry the cucumber slices with a paper towel before processing.

Dehydrated Okra

Preparation Time: 15 minutes
Dehydration Time: 12 hours
Servings: 4

Ingredients:

- 12 okra, sliced

Method:

1. Add the okra to the Cosori Premium Food Dehydrator.
2. Dry at 130 degrees F for 12 hours.

Storage Suggestions: Store in an airtight container.

Preparation & Dehydration Tips: Sprinkle with powdered herb or spice for added flavor.

Dried Sweet Potato

Preparation Time: 10 minutes
Dehydration Time: 12 hours
Servings: 4

Ingredients:

- 2 sweet potatoes
- 1 teaspoon onion powder

Method:

1. Season the sweet potato slices with onion powder.
2. Arrange in a single layer in the Cosori Premium Food Dehydrator.
3. Set at 115 degrees F.
4. Process for 12 hours.

Storage Suggestions: Store in a sealable plastic bag.

Preparation & Dehydration Tips: Use a mandolin slicer to prepare the sweet potatoes.

Dehydrated Beets

Preparation Time: 20 minutes
Dehydration Time: 12 hours
Servings: 4

Ingredients:

- 3 beets, sliced thinly
- ¼ cup water
- ¼ cup vinegar
- 1 tablespoon olive oil
- Salt to taste

Method:

1. Combine all the ingredients in a bowl.
2. Marinate for 10 minutes.
3. Arrange the beet slices in the Cosori Premium Food Dehydrator.
4. Dehydrate at 135 degrees F for 12 hours.

Storage Suggestions: Store in a sealable plastic bag.

Preparation & Dehydration Tips: Use a mandoliner slicer to slice the beets thinly.

Dehydrated Tomatoes

Preparation Time: 20 minutes
Dehydration Time: 8 hours
Servings: 2

Ingredients:

- 2 tomatoes, sliced into quarters
- Salt to taste

Method:

1. Add the tomatoes to the Cosori Premium Food Dehydrator.
2. Sprinkle with salt.
3. Set to 135 degrees F.
4. Process for 8 hours.

Storage Suggestions: Store in a sealable plastic bag. Squeeze out the air. Store for up to 2 months in a cool dry place. Freeze and store for up to 6 months.

Preparation & Dehydration Tips: Don't forget to scrape the seeds before drying.

Spiced Cucumbers

Preparation Time: 20 hours
Dehydration Time: 4 hours
Servings: 2

Ingredients:

- 2 cucumbers, sliced into rounds
- 2 teaspoons olive oil
- 2 teaspoons vinegar
- 1 tablespoon paprika
- 2 teaspoons onion powder
- 2 teaspoons garlic powder
- 2 teaspoons sugar
- Pinch chili powder

Method:

- Toss the cucumbers in oil and vinegar.
- Sprinkle with the sugar and spices.
- Put the cucumber slices in the Cosori Premium Food Dehydrator.
- Process at 135 degrees F for 6 hours.

Storage Suggestions: Store in an airtight container.

Preparation & Dehydration Tips: Dehydrate longer if you want your cucumber crispier.

Dehydrated Corn

Preparation Time: 10 minutes
Dehydration Time: 12 hours
Servings: 4

Ingredients:

- 8 cups corn kernels

Method:

1. Spread the corn kernels in the Cosori Premium Food Dehydrator.
2. Process at 125 degrees F for 12 hours.

Storage Suggestions: Store in a glass jar with lid.

Preparation & Dehydration Tips: You can also drizzle the corn kernels in olive oil before dehydrating.

Maple Carrot Straws

Preparation Time: 15 minutes
Dehydration Time: 6 hours
Servings: 4

Ingredients:

- 1 lb. carrots, sliced into long strips
- 1 tablespoon maple syrup
- 1 tablespoon olive oil
- Salt to taste

Method:

1. Combine all the ingredients in a bowl.
2. Arrange the strips in the Cosori Premium Food Dehydrator.
3. Process at 135 degrees F for 6 hours.

Storage Suggestions: Store in a food container.

Preparation & Dehydration Tips: Use a peeler to slice the carrots.

Dehydrated Asparagus

Preparation Time: 10 minutes
Dehydration Time: 6 hours
Servings: 2

Ingredients:

- 4 cups asparagus, trimmed and sliced

Method:

1. Arrange the asparagus in the Cosori Premium Food Dehydrator.
2. Process at 125 degrees F for 6 hours.

Storage Suggestions: Store in a sealable plastic bag.

Preparation & Dehydration Tips: You can also season the asparagus with salt or garlic powder.

Dehydrated Pizza Broccoli

Preparation Time: 15 minutes
Dehydration Time: 16 hours
Servings: 6

Ingredients:

- 3 cups broccoli florets
- 2 tomatoes, sliced in half
- 1 tablespoon dried basil
- 1 tablespoon dried oregano
- 2 cloves garlic, minced
- ¼ yellow onion, chopped
- 1 tablespoon smoked paprika
- 2 tablespoons tahini

Method:

1. Add all the broccoli florets to a bowl.
2. Blend the remaining ingredients in a food processor.
3. Pulse until smooth.
4. Toss the broccoli florets in the sauce.
5. Arrange the broccoli florets in the Cosori Premium Food Dehydrator.
6. Process at 135 degrees F for 16 hours.

Storage Suggestions: Store in an airtight container.

Preparation & Dehydration Tips: You can also use cauliflower for this recipe.

Spicy Garlic Kale

Preparation Time: 10 minutes
Dehydration Time: 6 hours
Servings: 4

Ingredients:

- 4 cups kale leaves, rinsed
- 2 tablespoons olive oil
- 1 tablespoon dried Sriracha
- ¼ teaspoon garlic powder
- Salt to taste

Method:

1. Arrange the kale leaves in the Cosori Premium Food Dehydrator.
2. Dry at 135 degrees F for 6 hours.
3. Toss in the olive oil.
4. Sprinkle with the remaining ingredients.

Storage Suggestions: Store in an airtight container.

Preparation & Dehydration Tips: Process for 8 hours if you want the kale leaves crispier.

Lemon Kale

Preparation Time: 15 minutes
Dehydration Time: 8 hours
Servings: 2

Ingredients:

- 2 cups kale leaves
- 1 tablespoon olive oil
- Salt to taste
- 1 teaspoon lemon juice

Method:

1. Toss the kale leaves in olive oil.
2. Season with the salt.
3. Arrange the kale leaves in the Cosori Premium Food Dehydrator.
4. Process at 135 degrees F for 8 hours.
5. Drizzle with lemon juice.

Storage Suggestions: Store in an airtight container for up to 5 days.

Preparation & Dehydration Tips: Dry the kale leaves thoroughly before processing.

Paprika Zucchini

Preparation Time: 10 minutes
Dehydration Time: 12 hours
Servings: 4

Ingredients:

- 2 zucchinis, sliced into rounds
- 1 tablespoon olive oil
- 1 teaspoon onion powder
- 1 teaspoon garlic powder
- 1 teaspoon paprika
- Salt and pepper to taste

Method:

1. Toss the zucchini in olive oil.
2. In another bowl, mix the onion powder, garlic powder, paprika, salt and pepper.
3. Add the zucchini to the Cosori Premium Food Dehydrator.
4. Dehydrate at 165 degrees F for 12 hours.

Storage Suggestions: Store in a sealed food container

Preparation & Dehydration Tips: You can also use this recipe to dehydrate eggplant.

Shawarma Kale

Preparation Time: 15 minutes
Dehydration Time: 13 hours
Servings: 4

Ingredients:

- 4 oz. kale, sliced
- 2 teaspoons olive oil
- Salt to taste
- 1 teaspoon cumin
- ¼ teaspoon ground cardamom
- ½ teaspoon smoked paprika
- ½ teaspoon ground coriander
- ½ teaspoon garlic powder
- ½ teaspoon cinnamon

Method:

1. Toss the kale in olive oil.
2. Stir in the salt and spices.
3. Arrange the kale in the Cosori Premium Food Dehydrator.
4. Dehydrate at 135 degrees F for 12 hours.

Storage Suggestions: Store in a glass jar with lid.

Preparation & Dehydration Tips: Massage the kale with the spices to infuse flavors.

Ranch Carrot

Preparation Time: 15 minutes
Dehydration Time: 12 hours
Servings: 6

Ingredients:

- 3 cups carrot strips
- 2 tablespoons water
- 1 packet ranch dressing seasoning powder

Method:

1. Soak the carrots in water.
2. Sprinkle with the ranch dressing seasoning.
3. Add the carrots to the Cosori Premium Food Dehydrator.
4. Dehydrate at 145 degrees F for 12 hours.

Storage Suggestions: Store in an airtight container.

Preparation & Dehydration Tips: Use a peeler to slice the carrots thinly.

Broccoli & Cashew Bites

Preparation Time: 15 minutes
Dehydration Time: 4 hours
Servings: 12

Ingredients:

- 2 ½ cups broccoli florets
- 2 ½ cups cashews
- ¼ cup onion, chopped
- 3 cloves garlic, crushed and minced
- 2 tablespoons olive oil
- 1 tablespoon jalapeno, chopped
- ¼ cup nutritional yeast
- Salt to taste

Method:

1. Add the broccoli and cashews to a blender or food processor.
2. Pulse until powdery.
3. Stir in the rest of the ingredients.
4. Pulse until smooth.
5. Form balls from the mixture.
6. Add these to the Cosori Premium Food Dehydrator.
7. Dry at 115 degrees F for 4 hours.

Storage Suggestions: Store in a food container and refrigerate for up to 1 week.

Preparation & Dehydration Tips: Soak cashews in water before processing in the blender.

Green Bean Crisps

Preparation Time: 10 minutes
Dehydration Time: 6 hours
Servings: 5

Ingredients:

- 2 lb. green beans
- 1 teaspoons olive oil
- Salt to taste

Method:

1. Coat the green beans with oil.
2. Sprinkle with the salt.
3. Spread it in the Cosori Premium Food Dehydrator.
4. Dehydrate at 115 degrees F for 6 hours.

Storage Suggestions: Store in a sealable plastic bag.

Preparation & Dehydration Tips: Trim the green beans before dehydrating.

Crunchy Green Peas

Preparation Time: 10 minutes
Dehydration Time: 8 hours
Servings: 4

Ingredients:

- 2 cups green peas, rinsed and drained
- 1 teaspoon olive oil
- Salt to taste

Method:

1. Dry the green peas with paper towels.
2. Add the green peas to a bowl.
3. Coat with oil.
4. Spread in the Cosori Premium Food Dehydrator.
5. Dry at 135 degrees F for 8 hours.
6. Sprinkle with salt before storing.

Storage Suggestions: Store in a glass jar with lid.

Preparation & Dehydration Tips: You can use green peas for this recipe.

Chapter 5: Herbs & Powder

Dried Basil Powder

Preparation Time: 10 minutes
Dehydration Time: 15 hours
Servings: 10 to 15

Ingredients:

- 3 cups basil leaves

Method:

1. Add the basil leaves to the Cosori Premium Food Dehydrator.
2. Dry at 105 degrees for 15 hours.
3. Grind the dried basil in a spice grinder or food processor.

Storage Suggestions: Store in an empty spice jar.

Preparation & Dehydration Tips: Use only fresh basil leaves.

Dried Herb Mix

Preparation Time: 15 minutes
Dehydration Time: 8 hours
Servings: 10 to 15

Ingredients:

- ½ cup thyme leaves
- ½ cup rosemary leaves
- 2 teaspoons lemon zest
- 6 cloves garlic, peeled

Method:

1. Combine all the ingredients in a food processor.
2. Pulse until smooth.
3. Spread the mixture in the Cosori Premium Food Dehydrator.
4. Dehydrate at 135 degrees F for 8 hours.

Storage Suggestions: Store in an empty spice bottle.

Preparation & Dehydration Tips: You can also add other herbs into the mix such as oregano or thyme.

Dried Parsley, Basil & Oregano Powder

Preparation Time: 15 minutes
Dehydration Time: 8 hours
Servings: 10 to 15

Ingredients:

- 2 tablespoons parsley leaves
- 2 tablespoons basil leaves
- 2 tablespoons oregano leaves
- 2 tablespoons brown sugar
- 2 tablespoons salt

Method:

1. Add the herb leaves to the Cosori Premium Food Dehydrator.
2. Dehydrate at 135 degrees F for 8 hours.
3. Transfer the dried leaves to a food processor.
4. Stir in the sugar and salt.

Storage Suggestions: Store in a mason jar with lid.

Preparation & Dehydration Tips: You can also skip the sugar and salt, and simply mix the dried herbs.

Garlic Powder

Preparation Time: 15 minutes
Dehydration Time: 12 hours
Servings: 24

Ingredients:

- 6 heads garlic, cloves separated, peeled and sliced

Method:

1. Spread the garlic slices in the Cosori Premium Food Dehydrator.
2. Dry at 125 degrees F for 12 hours.
3. Transfer the dried garlic into a blender or spice grinder.

Storage Suggestions: Sift the mixture before storing. Store the garlic powder in an airtight spice jar. Keep it in a cool and dry area.

Preparation & Dehydration Tips: You can also use a coffee grinder to grind the dried garlic.

Powdered Ginger

Preparation Time: 15 minutes
Dehydration Time: 8 hours
Servings: 10 to 15

Ingredients:

- 5 pieces ginger, sliced

Method:

1. Put the ginger in the Cosori Premium Food Dehydrator.
2. Dry at 95 degrees F for 8 hours.
3. Transfer the dried ginger to a food processor or spice grinder.
4. Grind the dried ginger into powder.

Storage Suggestions: Store in a mason jar.

Preparation & Dehydration Tips: Use a mandoliner slicer to slice the ginger.

Onion & Garlic Powder Mix

Preparation Time: 20 minutes
Dehydration Time: 12 hours
Servings:

Ingredients:

- 5 cloves garlic, peeled and sliced
- 1 onion, sliced

Method:

1. Place the garlic and onion slices in the Cosori Premium Food Dehydrator.
2. Dehydrate at 135 degrees F for 12 hours.
3. Transfer to a spice grinder.
4. Grind until powdery.

Storage Suggestions: Store in a mason jar.

Preparation & Dehydration Tips: Slice the onion and garlic thinly before dehydrating.

Kimchi Powder

Preparation Time: 5 minutes
Dehydration Time: 12 hours
Servings: 5

Ingredients:

- 2 cups kimchi

Method:

1. Add the kimchi to the Cosori Premium Food Dehydrator.
2. Dehydrate at 155 degrees F for 12 hours.
3. Add the dried kimchi to a spice grinder, blender or food processor.
4. Process until powdery.

Storage Suggestions: Store the powder in an empty spice jar.

Preparation & Dehydration Tips: Dehydrate longer if there is still moisture after 12 hours.

Onion Powder

Preparation Time: 10 minutes
Dehydration Time: 8 hours
Servings: 10 to 15

Ingredients:

- 5 onions, sliced

Method:

1. Arrange the onion slices in a single layer in the Cosori Premium Food Dehydrator.
2. Dehydrate at 145 degrees F for 8 hours.
3. Transfer the dried onion to a food processor.
4. Pulse until powdery.

Storage Suggestions: Store the onion powder in a mason jar.

Preparation & Dehydration Tips: Use a mandoline slicer to slice the onions thinly.

Tomato Powder

Preparation Time: 15 minutes
Dehydration Time: 12 hours
Servings: 10 to 15

Ingredients:

- Skins from 10 tomatoes

Method:

1. Add the tomato skins to a Cosori Premium Food Dehydrator.
2. Dry at 135 degrees F for 12 hours.
3. Transfer the dried tomatoes to a coffee grinder.
4. Grind until the mixture turns to powder.

Storage Suggestions: Store in a glass jar with lid.

Preparation & Dehydration Tips: You can also make tomato flakes from this recipe.

Leek Powder

Preparation Time: 5 minutes
Dehydration Time: 12 hours
Servings: 10 to 15

Ingredients:

- 4 cups leeks, sliced

Method:

1. Place the leeks in the Cosori Premium Food Dehydrator.
2. Dehydrate at 135 degrees F for 4 hours.
3. Put the dried leeks in a spice grinder.
4. Grind until powdery.

Storage Suggestions: Store in a tightly sealed food or spice container.

Preparation & Dehydration Tips: Do not use any browned parts of leeks.

Thyme, Garlic, Rosemary & Lemon Herb Mix

Preparation Time: 15 minutes
Dehydration Time: 8 hours
Servings: 15

Ingredients:

- ½ cup thyme leaves
- 6 cloves garlic, peeled
- ½ cup rosemary leaves
- 2 teaspoons lemon zest

Method:

1. Add all the ingredients to a food processor.
2. Pulse until well mixed.
3. Add the mixture to the Cosori Premium Food Dehydrator.
4. Dry at 135 degrees F for 8 hours.

Storage Suggestions: Store in a mason jar.

Preparation & Dehydration Tips: You can also use garlic powder in lieu of garlic slices with this recipe.

Parsley, Oregano, Basil, Thyme & Red Pepper Herb Mix

Preparation Time: 15 minutes
Dehydration Time: 8 hours
Servings: 15

Ingredients:

- 2 tablespoons fresh oregano leaves
- 2 tablespoons fresh parsley leaves
- 2 tablespoons fresh basil leaves
- 1 tablespoon fresh thyme leaves
- 1 teaspoon lemon zest
- 1 teaspoon red pepper, sliced

Method:

1. Combine all the ingredients in a bowl.
2. Add to the Cosori Premium Food Dehydrator.
3. Dehydrate at 135 degrees F for 8 hours.
4. After dehydrating the herbs and spices, transfer to a food processor.
5. Pulse until powdery.

Storage Suggestions: Store in a glass jar with lid.

Preparation & Dehydration Tips: You can also use red pepper flakes for this recipe.

Lemon Powder

Preparation Time: 30 minutes
Dehydration Time: 12 hours
Servings: 15

Ingredients:

- Peel from 6 lemons

Method:

1. Add the lemon peels to the Cosori Premium Food Dehydrator.
2. Dehydrate at 95 degrees F for 12 hours.
3. Transfer to a food processor.
4. Pulse until powdered.

Storage Suggestions: Store in sealable plastic bags.

Preparation & Dehydration Tips: You can stir in garlic powder for lemon garlic mix.

Mushroom Powder

Preparation Time: 15 minutes
Dehydration Time: 12 hours
Servings: 15

Ingredients:

- 2 cups shiitake mushrooms

Method:

1. Arrange the shiitake mushrooms in a single layer in the Cosori Premium Food Dehydrator.
2. Dry at 135 degrees F for 12 hours.
3. Place the dried mushrooms in a food processor.
4. Pulse until powdered.

Storage Suggestions: Store in a glass jar with lid. Place the jar in an area with low light.

Preparation & Dehydration Tips: You can also make this recipe using other types of mushrooms.

Porcini Cubes

Preparation Time: 20 minutes
Dehydration Time: 10 hours
Servings: 15

Ingredients:

- 2 oz. dried porcini mushrooms
- 2 teaspoons gelatin powder
- 3 tablespoons onion powder
- 2 tablespoons soy sauce
- 1 teaspoon fish sauce
- 1 tablespoon water
- 2 teaspoons salt

Method:

1. Combine all the ingredients in a bowl.
2. Form small balls from the mixture.
3. Shape into cubes.
4. Add the cubes to the Cosori Premium Food Dehydrator.
5. Dry at 125 degrees F for 10 hours.

Storage Suggestions: Wrap the cubes in foil and store in a cool dry place for up to 1 week.

Preparation & Dehydration Tips: Homemade onion powder gives the best results for this recipe.

Herbes de Provence

Preparation Time: 15 minutes
Dehydration Time: 8 hours
Servings: 15

Ingredients:

- 1 cup fresh basil leaves
- 1 cup fresh marjoram leaves
- 1 cup fresh rosemary leaves
- ½ cup fresh tarragon leaves
- ½ cup fresh thyme leaves
- ½ cup lavender buds
- 2 tablespoons dried savory

Method:

1. Add the fresh herbs to the Cosori Premium Food Dehydrator by batch. Do not overcrowd.
2. Dehydrate at 145 degrees F for 8 hours.
3. Transfer dried herbs to a food processor or spice grinder.
4. Grind until powdered.

Storage Suggestions: Store in a sealable plastic bag or glass jar with lid. Keep away from sunlight.

Preparation & Dehydration Tips: You can also use a coffee grinder to turn the spice mixture into powder.

Italian Seasoning Blend

Preparation Time: 15 minutes
Dehydration Time: 8 hours
Servings: 15

Ingredients:

- 1 cup fresh oregano leaves
- 1 cup fresh basil leaves
- 1 cup fresh thyme leaves
- ½ cup fresh sage leaves
- ½ cup fresh rosemary leaves

Method:

1. Arrange the fresh herb leaves in the Cosori Premium Food Dehydrator by batch.
2. Dehydrate at 145 degrees F for 8 hours.
3. Put the dried herbs in a food processor.
4. Pulse until powdered.

Storage Suggestions: Store in a glass jar. Keep the jar in a cool dry place.

Preparation & Dehydration Tips: You can also use a blender to turn the mixture into powder.

Taco Seasoning

Preparation Time: 15 minutes
Dehydration Time: 12 hours
Servings: 15

Ingredients:

- 1 cup oregano leaves
- 2 tablespoons ground cumin
- 2 tablespoons cayenne pepper
- 1 tablespoon onion powder
- 1 tablespoon garlic powder
- 1 tablespoon sweet paprika
- ½ teaspoon black pepper

Method:

1. Add the oregano leaves to the Cosori Premium Food Dehydrator.
2. Dehydrate at 145 degrees F for 12 hours.
3. Add to the spice grinder.
4. Grind until powdered.
5. Add the oregano powder in a glass jar.
6. Stir in the rest of the ingredients.
7. Shake to blend well.

Storage Suggestions: Seal the jar and keep away from sunlight.

Preparation & Dehydration Tips: Use freshly ground black pepper for this recipe.

Basil, Marjoram & Sage Herb Mix

Preparation Time: 15 minutes
Dehydration Time: 12 hours
Servings: 15

Ingredients:

- 1 cup fresh basil leaves
- 1 cup fresh marjoram leaves
- 1 cup fresh sage leaves

Method:

1. Place the fresh herbs in the Cosori Premium Food Dehydrator.
2. Dehydrate at 145 degrees F for 12 hours.
3. Transfer to a spice grinder.
4. Grind until powdered.

Storage Suggestions: Store in a glass jar with lid.

Preparation & Dehydration Tips: You can also add other herbs to this mixture.

Dried Herbs For Salad

Preparation Time: 15 minutes
Dehydration Time: 12 hours
Servings: 15

Ingredients:

- 1 cup parsley leaves
- ½ cup basil leaves
- ½ cup Parmesan cheese, grated
- 2 teaspoons paprika
- 2 teaspoons onion powder
- 2 teaspoons garlic powder
- Salt and pepper to taste

Method:

1. Place the parsley and basil leaves in the Cosori Premium Food Dehydrator.
2. Process at 145 degrees F for 12 hours.
3. Transfer to the spice grinder.

Storage Suggestions: Keep in an empty spice bottle.

Preparation & Dehydration Tips: Use homemade onion and garlic powder for this recipe.

Chapter 6: Crackers

Carrot Crackers

Preparation Time: 20 minutes
Dehydration Time: 10 hours
Servings: 10

Ingredients:

- 1 cup almonds, soaked overnight, rinsed, and drained
- 2 cups carrot pulp
- 1 tablespoon ground chia seeds
- 2 tablespoons ground flax seed
- 1 teaspoon Italian seasoning
- 1 tablespoon coconut aminos
- ½ teaspoon smoked paprika
- 1 tablespoon dried onion
- ½ teaspoon red pepper flakes
- 2 cups water

Method:

1. Add the almonds to a food processor or blender.
2. Pulse until crumbly.
3. Stir in the rest of the ingredients.
4. Pulse until fully combined.
5. Spread a thin layer of the dough in the Cosori Premium Food Dehydrator.
6. Dry at 125 degrees F for 2 hours.
7. Score the dough to form the crackers.
8. Dry at 115 degrees for 8 hours.

Storage Suggestions: Store in an airtight food container for up to 5 days.

Preparation & Dehydration Tips: Soak the almonds overnight the day before processing.

Green Crackers

Preparation Time: 20 minutes
Dehydration Time: 8 hours
Servings: 6

Ingredients:

- 1 cup green juice pulp
- ¼ cup ground flax seeds
- ¼ cup chia seeds
- ¼ cup nutritional yeast
- 2 tablespoons sesame seeds
- 1 tablespoon tamari
- ½ teaspoon salt
- ¼ cup water

Method:

1. Combine all the ingredients in a bowl.
2. Transfer to a food processor.
3. Pulse until fully combined.
4. Spread a thin layer of the mixture in the Cosori Premium Food Dehydrator.
5. Score the crackers.
6. Process at 115 degrees F for 5 hours.
7. Flip the crackers.
8. Dry for another 3 hours.

Storage Suggestions: Store in a sealable plastic bag for up to 7 days.

Preparation & Dehydration Tips: The mixture layer should be 1/8 inch thick only.

Seaweed & Tamari Crackers

Preparation Time: 15 minutes
Dehydration Time: 24 hours
Servings: 15

Ingredients:

- 1 cup flax seeds
- 2 nori sheets, broken
- 2 tablespoons tamari
- 1 ½ cups water

Method:

1. Mix all the ingredients in a bowl.
2. Spread a layer in the Cosori Premium Food Dehydrator.
3. Set it at 110 degrees F.
4. Process for 24 hours.
5. Break into crackers.

Storage Suggestions: Store in a glass jar with lid for up to 5 days.

Preparation & Dehydration Tips: Soak flaxseeds in water for 1 hour before processing.

Mexican Crackers

Preparation Time: 30 minutes
Dehydration Time: X hours
Servings: 15

Ingredients:

- ½ cup chia seeds
- 1 cup golden flaxseeds
- ½ cup pumpkin seeds
- ½ cup sunflower seeds
- 1 red bell pepper, chopped
- ¼ onion, chopped
- 1 cup carrot pulp
- 1 ½ teaspoons chipotle powder
- 1 teaspoon garlic powder
- Salt to taste
- ½ teaspoon cayenne pepper

Method:

1. Process the seeds in a blender or food processor until powdery.
2. Stir in the bell pepper and onion.
3. Pulse until smooth.
4. Stir in the rest of the ingredients.
5. Pulse until fully combined.
6. Spread the mixture in the Cosori Premium Food Dehydrator.
7. Score the crackers.
8. Dry at 115 degrees F for 6 hours.

Storage Suggestions: Store in a sealed food container for up to 5 days.

Preparation & Dehydration Tips: Soak the seeds in separate bowls of water for 6 hours before processing.

Flax Crackers

Preparation Time: 4 hours and 10 minutes
Dehydration Time: 24 hours
Servings: 12 crackers

Ingredients:

- 1 ½ cups water
- 1 clove garlic, minced
- ¾ cup golden flax seeds
- ¼ cup flax seeds
- 3 teaspoons sesame seeds, crushed
- 3 teaspoons poppy seeds, crushed
- 3 teaspoons garlic flakes
- 3 teaspoons onion flakes
- 3 teaspoons salt

Method:

1. Add the water and garlic in a blender.
2. Blend until smooth.
3. Pour the mixture in a bowl with the flaxseeds.
4. Soak for 4 hours.
5. Spread the gelatin mixture in the Cosori Premium Food Dehydrator.
6. Score the crackers with a knife.
7. Combine the remaining ingredients in a bowl.
8. Sprinkle the mixture on top of the crackers.
9. Process at 110 degrees F for 24 hours.

Storage Suggestions: Store in a glass jar with lid for up to 5 days.

Preparation & Dehydration Tips: Make your own garlic and onion flakes.

Sesame & Carrot Crackers

Preparation Time: 45 minutes
Dehydration Time: 24 hours
Servings: 15

Ingredients:

- 1 ½ cups of golden flaxseeds
- ¼ cup sesame seeds
- 2 cups carrot pulp
- 1 teaspoon of garlic powder
- ½ teaspoon of ground coriander
- 3 tablespoons tamari
- 1 cup water

Method:

1. Grind the flaxseeds in the spice grinder.
2. Add to a bowl along with the remaining ingredients.
3. Mix well.
4. Let sit for 30 minutes.
5. Spread the mixture in the Cosori Premium Food Dehydrator.
6. Process at 110 degrees F for 24 hours.

Storage Suggestions: Store in an airtight jar for up to 7 days.

Preparation & Dehydration Tips: Make your own garlic powder.

Onion & Nut Crackers

Preparation Time: 15 minutes
Dehydration Time: 12 hours
Servings: 12

Ingredients:

- 1 cup cashews
- 1 cup sunflower seeds
- ¼ cup coconut amino
- ½ cup water
- 1 clove garlic
- 1 green onion, chopped

Method:

1. Pulse all the ingredients in a food processor until fully combined.
2. Spread the mixture in the Cosori Premium Food Dehydrator.
3. Dehydrate at 115 degrees F for 1 hour.
4. Score the crackers.
5. Reduce temperature to 105 degrees F and process for another 11 hours.

Storage Suggestions: Store in an airtight container for up to 7 days.

Preparation & Dehydration Tips: You can also place a parchment paper sheet on top of the mixture and flatten with a rolling pin to make the layer thinner.

Peanut Butter & Banana Crackers

Preparation Time: 4 hours and 20 minutes
Dehydration Time: 6 hours
Servings: 12

Ingredients:

- 3 bananas, sliced
- ½ cup peanut butter
- ½ teaspoon cinnamon powder
- 1 cup ground peanuts
- 3 cups graham cracker crumbs

Method:

1. Mash the bananas and peanut butter in a bowl.
2. Stir in the rest of the ingredients.
3. Roll the dough into a large ball.
4. Flatten the ball to form a long rectangle.
5. Wrap the dough with wax paper and refrigerate for 4 hours.
6. Roll out the dough and slice.
7. Add the slices to the Cosori Premium Food Dehydrator.
8. Process at 145 degrees F for 6 hours.

Storage Suggestions: Store in a glass jar with lid for up to 5 days.

Preparation & Dehydration Tips: Do not skip refrigerating the dough before the dehydration process.

Tomato & Flaxseed Crackers

Preparation Time: 20 minutes
Dehydration Time: 8 hours
Servings: 24

Ingredients:

- 1 cup flaxseed
- 8sun-dried tomatoes
- 1 bell pepper, chopped
- 1tablespoon olive oil
- Salt to taste
- 2 tomatoes, chopped
- 1 onion, chopped
- 1 clove garlic, crushed through garlic press
- ¼ cup dried oregano leaves, crushed
- Salt and pepper to taste

Method:

1. Place the flaxseed in a bowl.
2. In another bowl, combine the remaining ingredients.
3. Stir in the flaxseeds.
4. Combine all the ingredients in the food processor.
5. Pulse until fully combined.
6. Spread the mixture in the Cosori Premium Food Dehydrator.
7. Process at 110 degrees F for 12 hours.

Storage Suggestions: Store in an airtight jar for up to 9 days.

Preparation & Dehydration Tips: Soak the flaxseeds in water for 2 hours before processing.

Seed Crackers

Preparation Time: X hours
Dehydration Time: X hours
Servings: 10

Ingredients:

- ¼ cup chia seeds
- ¾ cup flax seeds
- 1 cup water
- ¼ cup hemp seeds
- 1/3 cup sunflower seeds
- 2 tablespoons pumpkin seeds
- 1 tablespoon Italian seasoning
- Salt and pepper to taste

Method:

1. Soak the chia seeds and flax seeds in water for 1 hour.
2. Drain.
3. Transfer to a bowl.
4. Stir in the rest of the ingredients.
5. Process at 115 degrees F for 90 minutes.
6. Flip and break into smaller pieces.
7. Dry at 105 degrees F for 8 hours.

Storage Suggestions: Store in an airtight container for up to 7 days.

Preparation & Dehydration Tips: Serve with hummus.

Chapter 7: Sweets & Desserts

Oatmeal Raisin Cookies

Preparation Time: 15 minutes
Dehydration Time: 12 hours
Servings: 6

Ingredients:

- 1 cup quick rolled oats
- 1 cup pecans
- ¼ cup pumpkin seeds
- ¾ cup raisins
- 2 tablespoons coconut oil
- ¼ cup maple syrup
- ¼ teaspoon ground ginger
- ½ teaspoon ground cinnamon
- ¼ teaspoon ground clove
- ¼ teaspoon ground allspice
- Salt to taste

Method:

1. Mix all the ingredients in a food processor.
2. Pulse until fully combined.
3. Form balls from the mixture.
4. Flatten the balls and place in the Cosori Premium Food Dehydrator.
5. Dehydrate at 160 degrees F for 12 hours.
6. Let cool in a tray.

Storage Suggestions: Store cookies in an airtight container for up to 6 days.

Preparation & Dehydration Tips: Let cookies cool for at least 8 hours.

Almond Choco Cookies

Preparation Time: 15 minutes
Dehydration Time: 12 hours
Servings: 10

Ingredients:

- 1 cup almond butter
- 1 cup coconut flakes
- ½ cup pistachios
- ½ cup chocolate chips

Method:

1. Combine all the ingredients in a food processor.
2. Pulse until fully combined.
3. Form balls from the mixture.
4. Flatten with a spoon to form the cookies.
5. Add the cookies to the Cosori Premium Food Dehydrator.
6. Dehydrate at 160 degrees F for 12 hours.

Storage Suggestions: Store in a cookie jar with lid. Consume within 3 days.

Preparation & Dehydration Tips: Let cool for at least 8 hours before serving.

Almond & Raisins Cookies

Preparation Time: 15 minutes
Dehydration Time: 12 hours
Servings: 12

Ingredients:

- 1 cup almond butter
- 1 cup coconut flakes
- ½ cup walnuts, chopped
- ½ cup raisins

Method:

1. Stir all the ingredients in a food processor.
2. Pulse until fully combined.
3. Form cookies from the mixture.
4. Place the cookies in the Cosori Premium Food Dehydrator.
5. Process at 160 degrees F for 12 hours.
6. Let cool and serve.

Storage Suggestions: Store in a glass jar with lid. Consume within 5 days.

Preparation & Dehydration Tips: Cool on a tray for 8 hours before storing or serving.

Choco Cashew Cookies

Preparation Time: 15 minutes
Dehydration Time: 12 hours
Servings: 12

Ingredients:

- 2 cups cashews
- ¼ cup maple syrup
- ½ cup cocoa powder
- ½ teaspoon ground cinnamon
- 1 teaspoon vanilla extract
- ¼ teaspoon ground nutmeg
- Salt to taste

Method:

1. Add all the ingredients to a food processor.
2. Pulse until fully combined.
3. Form cookies from the mixture.
4. Place the cookies in the Cosori Premium Food Dehydrator.
5. Dehydrate at 160 degrees F for 12 hours.

Storage Suggestions: Store in a cookie jar. Consume within 7 days.

Preparation & Dehydration Tips: Use unsalted cashews for this recipe.

Vegan Cookie

Preparation Time: 15 minutes
Dehydration Time: 6 hours
Servings: 12

Ingredients:

- 2 apples, chopped
- 4 tablespoons flax seeds
- 1 teaspoon ground cinnamon
- ½ cup almonds
- ½ cup dates
- 4 cup oats

Method:

1. Combine the ingredients in a food processor.
2. Pulse until fully combined.
3. Form cookies from the mixture.
4. Dry at 113 degrees F for 4 hours.
5. Flip and cook for another 2 hours.

Storage Suggestions: Store in an airtight cookie jar. Consume within 12 days.

Preparation & Dehydration Tips: Sprinkle with a little sugar before flipping.

Watermelon Candy

Preparation Time: 10 minutes
Dehydration Time: 8 hours
Servings: 30

Ingredients:

- 1 ½ watermelon, sliced into strips
- 1 tablespoon sugar

Method:

1. Arrange the watermelon strips in the Cosori Premium Food Dehydrator.
2. Process at 125 degrees F for 8 hours.

Storage Suggestions: Wrap in waxed paper and store in a cool dry place for up to 3 days.

Preparation & Dehydration Tips: You can skip the sugar if you want to cut back on sugar.

Dried Marshmallows

Preparation Time: 5 minutes
Dehydration Time: 3 hours
Servings: 12

Ingredients:

- 8 cups marshmallows

Method:

1. Arrange the marshmallows in a single layer in the Cosori Premium Food Dehydrator.
2. Set it to 160 degrees F.
3. Process for 3 hours.

Storage Suggestions: Store in an airtight food container. Consume within 3 days.

Preparation & Dehydration Tips: Drizzle with chocolate syrup before serving.

Rhubarb Candy

Preparation Time: 1 hour and 30 minutes
Dehydration Time: 12 hours
Servings: 12

Ingredients:

- ½ cup water
- 2 cups sugar
- 4 stalks rhubarb, trimmed and sliced

Method:

1. Pour the water into a saucepan over medium heat.
2. Stir in the sugar.
3. Heat until the sugar has been dissolved.
4. Coat the rhubarb in the syrup.
5. Let sit for 1 hour.
6. Place the rhubarb in the Cosori Premium Food Dehydrator.
7. Process at 135 degrees F for 12 hours.

Storage Suggestions: Store in the freezer, wrapped in waxed paper for up to 3 months.

Preparation & Dehydration Tips: You can also soak the rhubarb in honey instead of the syrup.

Strawberry & Beetroot Candy

Preparation Time: 15 minutes
Dehydration Time: 24 hours
Servings: 12

Ingredients:

- 2 cups date paste
- ¼ cup beetroot juice
- 1 teaspoon strawberry extract

Method:

1. Combine all the ingredients in a bowl.
2. Form several strips from the mixture.
3. Arrange the strips in the Cosori Premium Food Dehydrator.
4. Process at 115 degrees F for 24 hours.

Storage Suggestions: Store in an airtight container.

Preparation & Dehydration Tips: Let cool for at least 3 hours before storing.

Apricot cookies

Preparation Time: 20 minutes
Dehydration Time: 6 hours
Servings: 12

Ingredients:

- 1 cup peanut butter
- 2 cup dates, pitted and sliced
- 1 cup dried apricots
- 1 cup coconut flakes
- ¼ cup water

Method:

1. Combine all the ingredients in the food processor.
2. Pulse until fully combined.
3. Form cookies from the mixture.
4. Add these to the Cosori Premium Food Dehydrator.
5. Dehydrate at 145 degrees F for 6 hours.

Storage Suggestions: Store in a sealed cookie jar.

Preparation & Dehydration Tips: Let cool before storing in the cookie jar.

Chapter 8: Chips

Garlic Zucchini Chips

Preparation Time: 15 minutes
Dehydration Time: 4 hours
Servings: 4

Ingredients:

- 3 zucchinis, sliced into thin rounds
- 2 tablespoons olive oil
- 2 tablespoons sesame seeds
- 2 tablespoons dried thyme, crushed
- 2 cloves garlic, grated
- Salt to taste

Method:

1. Coat the zucchini with olive oil.
2. Sprinkle with the sesame seeds, thyme, garlic and salt.
3. Add these to the Cosori Premium Food Dehydrator.
4. Dehydrate at 158 degrees F for 2 hours.
5. Flip and dry for another 2 hours.

Storage Suggestions: Store in a sealable plastic bag.

Preparation & Dehydration Tips: Before dehydrating, press the zucchini rounds with paper towel to remove excess moisture.

Pear Chips

Preparation Time: 10 minutes
Dehydration Time: 10 hours
Servings: 10

Ingredients:

- 10 pears, cored and sliced thinly

Method:

1. Arrange the pear slices in the Cosori Premium Food Dehydrator.
2. Dehydrate at 145 degrees F for 8 hours.

Storage Suggestions: Store in a sealed food container for up to 7 days.

Preparation & Dehydration Tips: Make sure the pear slices do not overlap to ensure even crisp.

Banana Chips

Preparation Time: 15 minutes
Dehydration Time: 12 hours
Servings: 4

Ingredients:

- 4 bananas, sliced thinly
- 1 teaspoon lemon juice

Method:

1. Drizzle the banana slices with lemon juice.
2. Add these to the Cosori Premium Food Dehydrator.
3. Process at 135 degrees F for 12 hours.

Storage Suggestions: Store in a vacuum sealed plastic for up to 3 months.

Preparation & Dehydration Tips: Drizzling bananas with lemon juice prevents browning.

Sweet Potato Chips

Preparation Time: 15 minutes
Dehydration Time: 4 hours
Servings: 2

Ingredients:

- 2 sweet potatoes, scrubbed and sliced thinly
- Salt to taste
- 2 teaspoons onion powder

Method:

1. Arrange the sweet potatoes in the Cosori Premium Food Dehydrator.
2. Process at 155 degrees F for 2 hours.
3. Flip and dry for another 2 hours.
4. Sprinkle with salt and onion powder.

Storage Suggestions: Store in a sealable plastic bag.

Preparation & Dehydration Tips: Use homemade onion powder.

Apple Chips with Cinnamon

Preparation Time: 15 minutes
Dehydration Time: 8 hours
Servings: 4

Ingredients:

- 4 apples, sliced thinly
- ¼ cup sugar
- 1 tablespoon ground cinnamon

Method:

1. Mix the cinnamon and sugar.
2. Coat the apple slices with this mixture.
3. Place the apple slices in the Cosori Premium Food Dehydrator.
4. Process at 135 degrees F for 12 hours.

Storage Suggestions: Store in an airtight food container.

Preparation & Dehydration Tips: Use a mandoliner slicer to slice the apples thinly.

Chapter 9: Soup

Dried Beef Soup Bouillion

Preparation Time: 15 minutes
Dehydration Time: 48 hours
Servings: 20

Ingredients:

- 2 gallons beef broth

Method:

1. Pour the beef broth into the dehydrator sheets of the Cosori Premium Food Dehydrator.
2. Dehydrate at 140 degrees F for 24 hours.
3. Flip and dehydrate for another 24 hours.

Storage Suggestions: Break and wrap smaller pieces in waxed paper. Store for up to 3 weeks.

Preparation & Dehydration Tips: You can also dehydrate longer for up to 48 hours per run.

Chicken Soup Bouillion

Preparation Time: 15 minutes
Dehydration Time: 48 hours
Servings: 10

Ingredients:

- 1-gallon chicken broth

Method:

1. Add the broth to the dehydrator sheet.
2. Process at 140 degrees F for 24 hours.
3. Flip and then process for another 24 hours.

Storage Suggestions: Break the broth sheet into smaller pieces before storing individually by wrapping with waxed paper.

Preparation & Dehydration Tips: Dehydrate longer for up to 48 hours per run.

Tomato Soup Dried mix

Preparation Time: 15 minutes
Dehydration Time: 12 hours
Servings: 4

Ingredients:

- 2 cups tomatoes, sliced
- 1 tablespoons onion powder
- 1 teaspoon dried thyme
- ½ teaspoon dried sage
- Salt to taste

Method:

1. Dehydrate the tomatoes in the Cosori Premium Food Dehydrator for 12 hours.
2. Add the dehydrated tomatoes to a food processor.
3. Process until powdery.
4. Stir in the rest of the ingredients.
5. Pulse until fully combined.

Storage Suggestions: Store in an airtight container.

Preparation & Dehydration Tips: To serve, mix 3 tablespoons tomato soup powder with 6 ounces hot water.

Taco Stew

Preparation Time: 1 hour
Dehydration Time: 12 hours
Servings: 4

Ingredients:

- 1 tablespoon olive oil
- 1 onion, chopped
- 2 red bell pepper, chopped
- 2 lb. ground turkey
- 12 oz. sweet corn, drained
- 14 oz. canned diced tomatoes
- 14 oz. black beans, rinsed and drained
- 1 packet taco spice mix
- Salt to taste

Method:

1. Pour the olive oil into a pan over medium heat.
2. Cook the onion, bell pepper and ground turkey for 5 minutes.
3. Drain and then put the mixture back to the pan.
4. Stir in the rest of the ingredients.
5. Bring to a boil.
6. Reduce heat and simmer for 30 minutes.
7. Let cool.
8. Spread the mixture in the Cosori Premium Food Dehydrator.
9. Process at 145 degrees F for 12 hours.

Storage Suggestions: Divide dried soup mix into several sealable bags. Each should have 1 cup powder.

Preparation & Dehydration Tips: You can also use ground beef in place of ground turkey if you like.

Vegetable Stock

Preparation Time: 15 minutes
Dehydration Time: 15 hours
Servings: 2

Ingredients:

- 1 onion, sliced
- 4 garlic cloves, peeled
- 1 tablespoon fresh ginger strips
- 1 parsnip, sliced
- 3 celery ribs, chopped
- 2 carrots, sliced
- 1 leek, sliced
- 10 mushrooms
- Salt to taste

Method:

1. Add all the vegetables in the Cosori Premium Food Dehydrator.
2. Process at 145 degrees F for 15 hours.
3. Let cool.
4. Transfer to a food processor.
5. Pulse until powdery.
6. Stir in the salt.
7. Pulse until fully combined.

Storage Suggestions: Store in a glass jar with lid for up to 3 months.

Preparation & Dehydration Tips: Make sure that the vegetables do not overlap. If necessary, dehydrate in batches.

Chapter 10: Dairy

Cheese Powder

Preparation Time: 20 minutes
Dehydration Time: 15 hours
Servings: 2

Ingredients:

- 1 block hard cheese (Parmesan, Gruyere, Cheddar), sliced

Method:

1. Add the cheese slices to the Cosori Premium Food Dehydrator.
2. Process at 145 degrees F for 15 hours.
3. Transfer the dehydrated cheese to a food processor.
4. Pulse until powdery.

Storage Suggestions: Store the cheese powder in a large spice bottle. Keep refrigerated.

Preparation & Dehydration Tips: Slice the cheese as thinly as possible to dehydrate faster.

Ground Cottage Cheese

Preparation Time: 15 minutes
Dehydration Time: 15 hours
Servings: 1

Ingredients:

- 2 cups cottage cheese

Method:

1. Spread the cottage cheese in the Cosori Premium Food Dehydrator.
2. Dry at 145 degrees F for 15 hours.

Storage Suggestions: Store in an airtight and watertight glass jar with lid.

Preparation & Dehydration Tips: You can also use other soft cheeses for this recipe.

Yogurt Drop

Preparation Time: 30 minutes
Dehydration Time: 8 hours
Servings: 2

Ingredients:

- ¾ cup yogurt
- 1 egg white

Method:

1. Use a hand mixer to beat the eggs until you see stiff peaks forming.
2. Stir in the yogurt.
3. Mix until fully combined.
4. Add the yogurt mixture to a piping bag.
5. Squeeze the piping bag to release small drops in the Cosori Premium Food Dehydrator.
6. Dehydrate at 125 degrees F for 8 hours.

Storage Suggestions: Store in a glass jar with lid. Consume within 5 days.

Preparation & Dehydration Tips: You can also use flavored yogurt for this recipe.

Yogurt Leather

Preparation Time: 15 minutes
Dehydration Time: 8 hours
Servings: 3

Ingredients:

- 3 cups yogurt

Method:

1. Spread the yogurt in the Cosori Premium Food Dehydrator.
2. Process at 125 degrees F for 8 hours.

Storage Suggestions: Slice into strips. Wrap each strip with waxed paper.

Preparation & Dehydration Tips: Sprinkle with sugar if you want to sweet it a bit.

Dried Feta

Preparation Time: 15 minutes
Dehydration Time: 12 hours
Servings: 2

Ingredients:

- 3 cups feta cheese, sliced into cubes

Method:

1. Arrange the feta cheese cubes in the Cosori Premium Food Dehydrator.
2. Dehydrate at 145 degrees F for 15 hours.

Storage Suggestions: Vacuum seal the dried cheese and store it for up to 6 months.

Preparation & Dehydration Tips: You can also slice the feta cheese into strips.

Chapter 11: Flour

Pumpkin Flour

Preparation Time: 15 minutes
Dehydration Time: 8 hours
Servings: 2

Ingredients:

- 4 cups pumpkin puree

Method:

1. Spread the pureed pumpkin in the Cosori Premium Food Dehydrator.
2. Process at 125 degrees F for 8 hours.
3. Transfer to a coffee grinder.
4. Grind until powdery.

Storage Suggestions: Store in an airtight jar for up to 5 years.

Preparation & Dehydration Tips: You can also use pureed squash for this recipe.

Corn Flour

Preparation Time: 15 minutes
Dehydration Time: 12 hours
Servings: 2

Ingredients:

- 8 cups corn kernels

Method:

1. Spread the corn kernels in the Cosori Premium Food Dehydrator.
2. Process at 145 degrees F for 12 hours.
3. Transfer the dried corn in a food processor or coffee grinder.
4. Grind until powdery.

Storage Suggestions: Store the flour in an airtight glass jar.

Preparation & Dehydration Tips: Do not overcrowd the dehydrator. If necessary, process the corn kernels by batch.

Sweet Potato Flour

Preparation Time: 15 minutes
Dehydration Time: 10 hours
Serving: 1

Ingredients:

- 6 sweet potatoes, sliced into thin strips
- Water

Method:

1. Add the sweet potato strips to a pot of water.
2. Boil for 15 minutes or until tender.
3. Mash the sweet potatoes.
4. Spread a thin layer of the mashed sweet potatoes in the Cosori Premium Food Dehydrator.
5. Dehydrate at 135 degrees F for 6 hours.
6. Transfer to a food processor.
7. Pulse until powdery.

Storage Suggestions: Store in a glass jar with lid.

Preparation & Dehydration Tips: You can make the mashed potatoes a day ahead prior to processing.

Sprouted Grain Flour

Preparation Time: 15 minutes
Dehydration Time: 12 hours
Serving: 1

Ingredients:

- 4 cups sprouted grains

Method:

1. Spread a thin layer of the grains in the Cosori Premium Food Dehydrator.
2. Process at 113 degrees F for 12 hours.
3. Pour the dried grains into a food processor.
4. Pulse until powdery.

Storage Suggestions: Store in a glass jar with lid. Use within a month.

Preparation & Dehydration Tips: Dry the sprouted grains with paper towel before placing in the dehydrator.

Chickpea Flour

Preparation Time: 15 minutes
Dehydration Time: 8 hours
Serving: 1

Ingredients:

- 4 cups chickpeas, rinsed and drained

Method:

1. Dry the chickpeas in your Cosori Premium Food Dehydrator at 145 degrees F for 8 hours.
2. Place the dried chickpeas in a blender.
3. Pulse until powdery.

Storage Suggestions: Store the chickpea flour in an airtight food container.

Preparation & Dehydration Tips: Dry the chickpeas thoroughly before processing.

Conclusion

Dehydration is an excellent way to make healthy snack alternatives and support in leading a healthier lifestyle.

If you often find yourself buying a lot of dried produce and food items, then getting a dehydrator would be a terrific choice for you.

Buying and utilizing seasonal produce to make your own snacks, treats, and condiments will greatly minimize your spending in the long run as you can create and store food to use for a longer period of time.

One notable benefit is that you can buy fruits and vegetables in bulk when they are in season and rehydrate them whenever you like. You'll surely love the COSORI Premium Food Dehydrator if you're constantly throwing away degraded food. You can now save fresh produce from ending up in the trash since you can simply dehydrate your excess supply.

Dehydration also allows you to keep more food but with much less space. They are easier to carry and transport, particularly when you're camping in remote areas and do not have any access to most ingredients.

They don't even require freezing, so it saves you in electricity costs too. Furthermore, unlike canning and other methods of food preservation, it retains more of the essential nourishment.

Also, cooking becomes enjoyable due to the reduced preparation time.

Cheers to more convenient food preparations!

Printed in the USA
CPSIA information can be obtained
at www.ICGtesting.com
LVHW070026110124
768241LV00076B/2885

9 781953 702906